Life before Birth

The s ... ıths

Text Stephen Parker   **Illustrations** John Bavosi

British Museum (Natural History)
Cambridge University Press

Published by the British Museum (Natural History), London
and the Syndics of the Cambridge University Press
The Pitt Building, Trumpington Street, Cambridge CB2 1RP
Bentley House, 200 Euston Road, London NW1 2DB
32 East 57th Street, New York, NY 10022, USA
296 Beaconsfield Parade, Middle Park, Melbourne 3206, Australia

© Trustees of the British Museum (Natural History) 1979

First Published 1979. Reprinted 1983

Printed in Great Britain by Valance Press Ltd, London W3.

ISBN 0 521 22382 2 hard covers
ISBN 0 521 29464 9 paperback

Library of Congress Cataloguing in Publication Data

Parker, Stephen
    Life before birth.

    'Adapted from a slide-sound programme of the same name
in the Hall of Human Biology at the British Museum
(Natural History), London.'
    SUMMARY: Describes human growth and development from
fertilization to the birth nine months later.
    1. Fetus. 2. Embryology, Human. [1. Fetus.
2. Embryology, Human]. I. Bavosi, John. II. British Museum
(Natural History). III. Title.
RG600.P37   612.6'47   78-60029

Contents

Preface

Life Before Birth tells the story of the first nine months of a human life. Nine months spent growing and developing from a tiny cell, smaller than a pinhead, into a fully formed baby. It does not deal with side issues, complications or abnormalities. Details of these can be found in medical textbooks.

Life Before Birth is adapted from a slide-sound programme of the same name in the Hall of Human Biology, at the British Museum (Natural History). It was developed originally as an integral part of the successful exhibition *Human Biology – An Exhibition of Ourselves*, opened in May 1977.

Part one

in which the sperm cell fertilizes the egg
cell, and a new life begins

Introduction

All human beings begin in the same way. A sperm cell from the father joins with an egg cell (**ovum**) from the mother to form a single cell, the fertilized egg.

The fertilized egg is smaller than a pinhead, but inside it, in the chromosomes, are all the instructions and information needed for a new human being to develop.

The egg cell

Egg cells are stored in the two **ovaries** of the woman. There are many thousands of egg cells in each ovary, but only one ripens and is released each month.

The egg cell travels along the **oviduct** towards the **uterus** (the womb). It is while the egg is in the oviduct that it might be fertilized by a sperm cell. If there are no sperm cells present, the egg cell reaches the uterus and is lost. The lining of the uterus, which is thick and well supplied with blood, also breaks down and is lost during the monthly **menstruation** (the 'period').

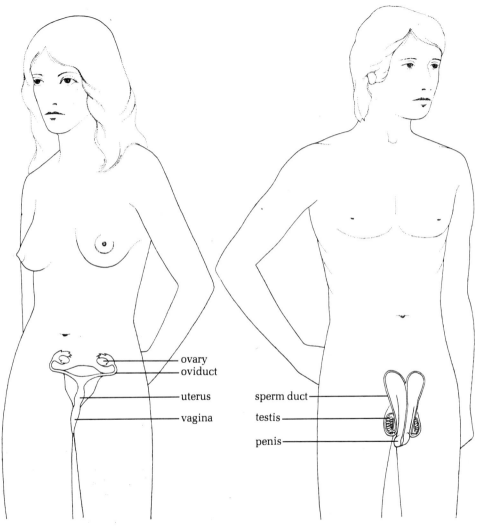

ovary
oviduct

uterus

vagina

sperm duct

testis

penis

The sperm cell

Sperm cells are minute, tadpole-shaped cells made in the two **testes** of the man. During sexual intercourse, the man places his **penis** in the **vagina** of the woman. Many millions of sperm cells are released (**ejaculated**) by the man, and enter the vagina of the woman.

As the sperm cells make their way through the uterus, many are lost. Many more take the wrong turning and swim into the empty oviduct. Only a few manage to reach the oviduct where the egg is waiting, and only one of the millions originally released will fertilize the egg cell.

Here is the egg cell in the oviduct, surrounded by sperm cells which have managed to complete the long journey. One of the sperm cells has bored its way through the jelly-like coating around the egg cell. It is this sperm that will fertilize the egg.

For the other sperm cells the journey has been in vain, and they soon die.

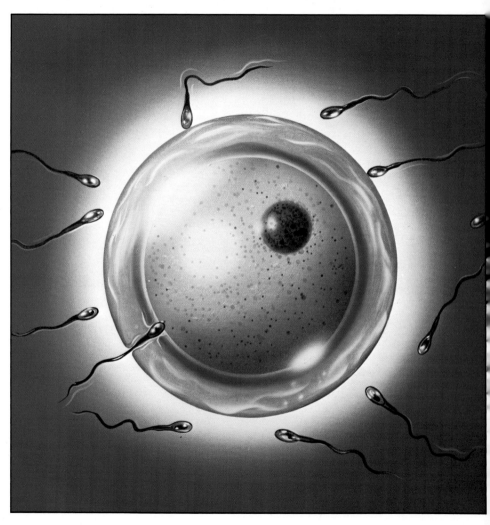

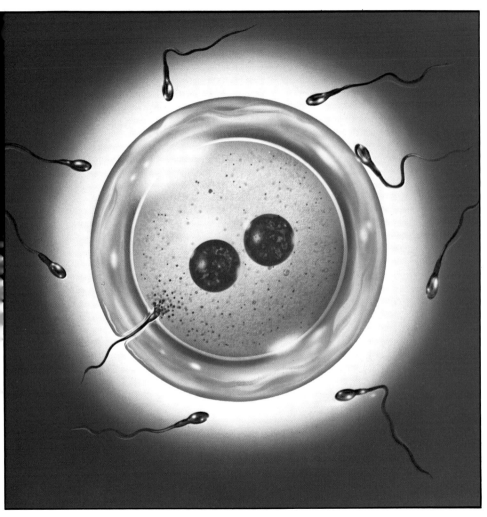

The head of the sperm cell detaches from the tail, and swells as it approaches the nucleus of the egg cell. The head of the sperm cell contains a set of 23 chromosomes from the father. The nucleus of the egg cell contains a set of 23 chromosomes from the mother. The next step is to bring these two sets of chromosomes together.

Fertilization

The head of the sperm cell releases its chromosomes, which look like short pieces of thread. The egg cell nucleus also releases its chromosomes, and both sets line up in the middle of the cell. This is the moment of fertilization, when a new life comes into being.

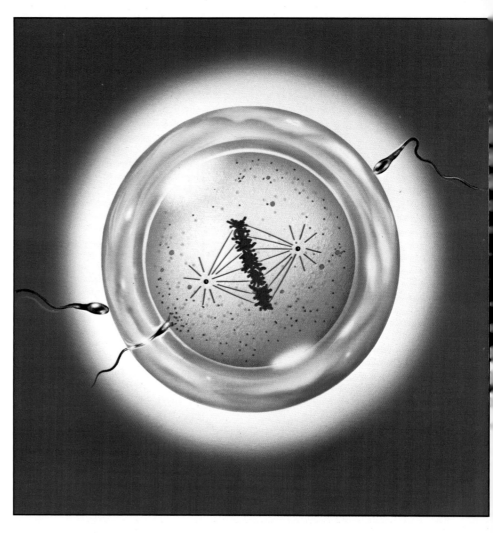

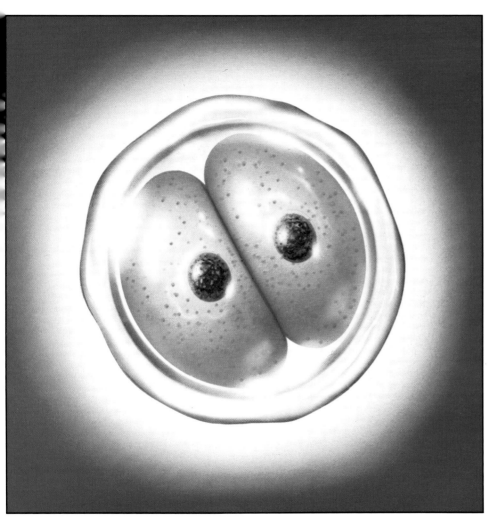

The fertilized egg, which now has a complete double-set of 46 chromosomes, moves slowly along the oviduct towards the uterus. A few hours after fertilization, it divides into two smaller cells. A few hours after this, each of the two cells divides, forming four cells, then eight cells, and so on.

Before each cell division, all the chromosomes are copied, so that each new cell receives a complete double-set.

At the eight-cell stage, the cells are still surrounded by the jelly-like coating. As they are swept along the oviduct, the cells continue to divide and gradually they get smaller and smaller.

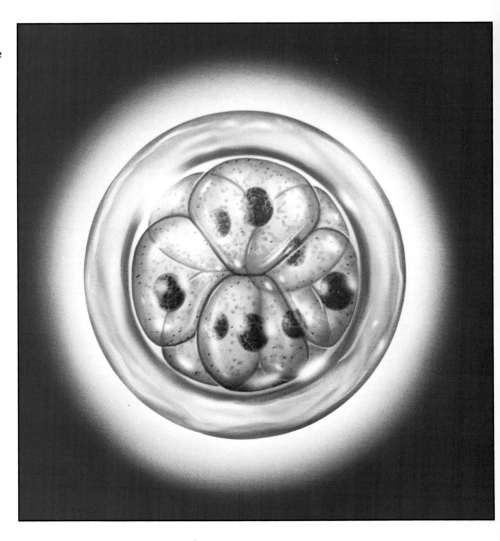

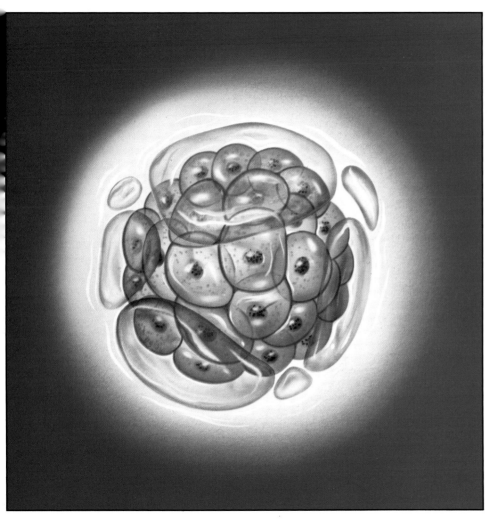

Three or four days after fertilization, the jelly-like coating begins to break down. By now there are about forty cells, some on the outside of the ball and some on the inside. A few of the outer cells have started to divide more frequently than the others. These are the first signs of differences between the cells, and they will have important consequences, as we shall soon see.

The ball of cells reaches the uterus about five days after fertilization. There are now over one hundred cells, of two main kinds. The large flattened cells on the **outside** of the ball will form the placenta and the membranes that surround and protect the baby while it is in the uterus. It is the small group of cells **inside** the ball that will develop into the baby.

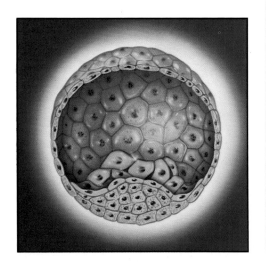

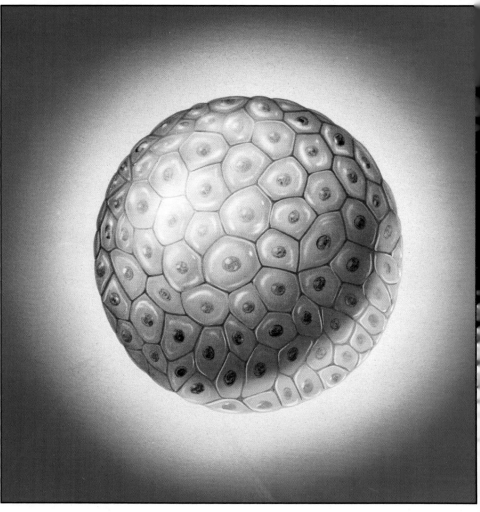

Part two

in which the ball of cells develops into a
recognizable human foetus.

Inside the uterus

About a week after fertilization, the ball of cells touches down on the inner lining of the uterus. The lining is thick and well supplied with blood vessels, ready to nourish the ball of cells as it burrows in. The cells in the ball are still dividing, becoming smaller and smaller. However, the original egg cell was so large that the cells in the ball are now back to normal cell size.

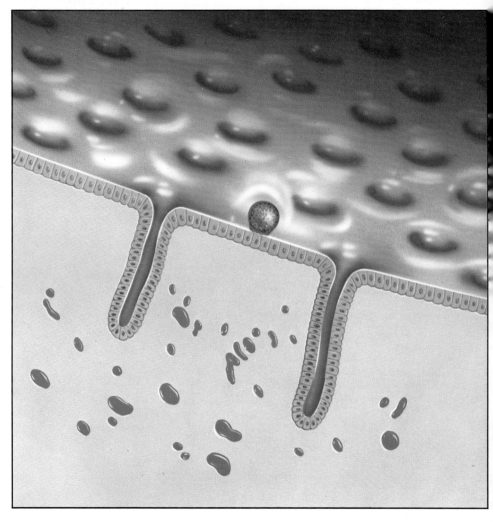

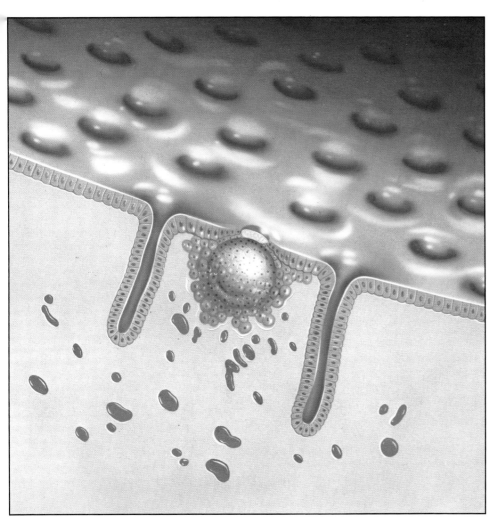

The ball of cells has been living on stored nutrients for the past week. As it burrows into the lining of the uterus, special cells on the outside of the ball eat their way into the lining, absorbing nutrients from the mother's cells and passing them to the inner cells.

The new supply of nutrients and building materials means that the cells can increase in size before dividing, and the ball of cells starts to grow.

About eight or nine days after fertilization, the ball of cells has burrowed right into the lining of the uterus. The inner cells have arranged themselves into two arch-shaped layers, while the outer cells continue to eat their way into the lining to obtain nutrients. Nobody fully understands why the tissue of the mother's uterus does not reject the ball of cells, which is in effect a 'foreign body'.

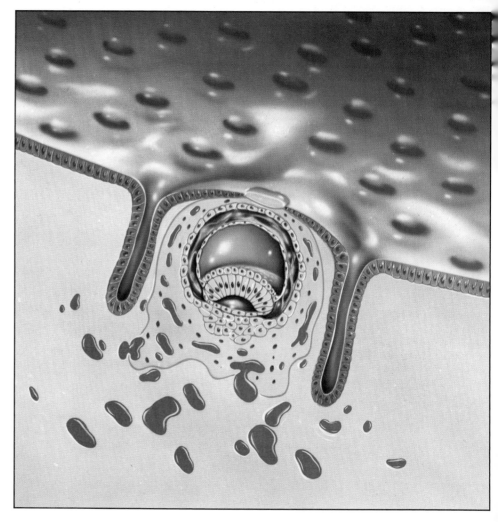

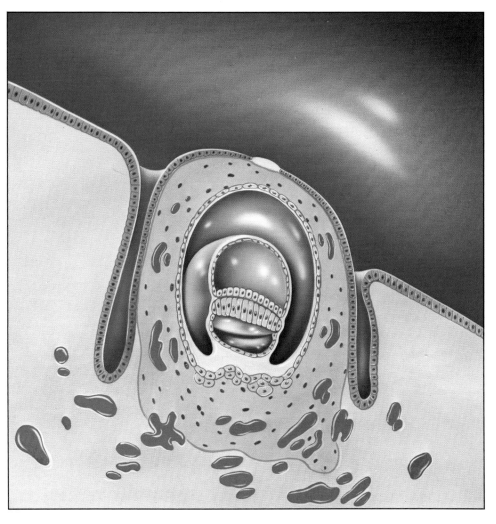

The ball of cells is still only 1 mm across, but it is made up of several hundred cells of different shapes and sizes, each cell with its own job to do.

The two cell layers inside the ball have become flat and disc shaped. It is this two-layered **disc** of cells that will form the baby.

About twelve days after fertilization, a **streak** appears on the underside of the disc. This streak is also seen in the early embryos of other mammals, and in the embryos of birds, fish, and many other animals. It signals the beginning of a very important phase in the development of the embryo. The cells are extremely active during this phase, dividing and growing and moving into position.

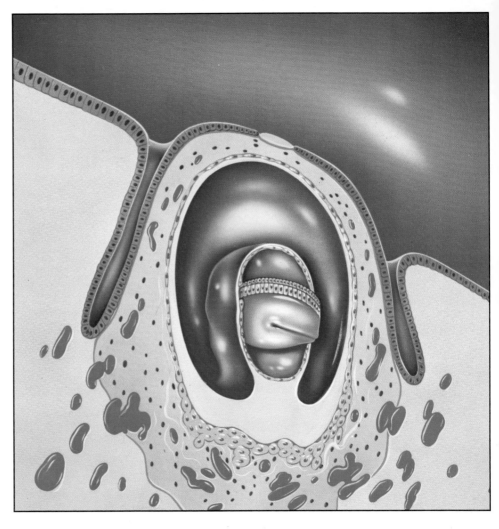

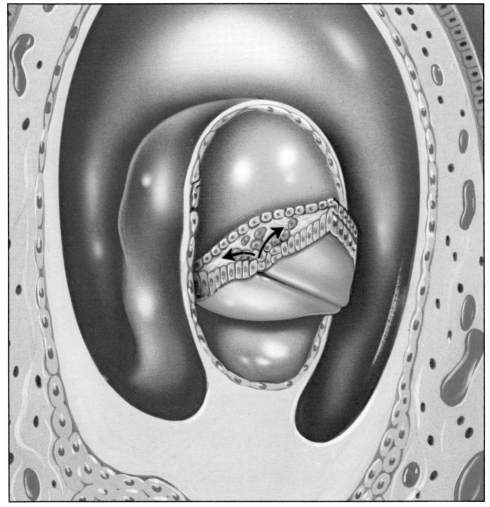

Taking a closer look inside the disc, we see the cause of the streak. The cells in the lower layer are dividing, growing and pushing their way in between the other cells to form a third layer. The **three-layered** organization of the early embryo is very important. Each cell layer is destined to form certain parts of the body, as you can see on the next page.

Three layers of the body

As development continues, the three-layered disc of cells will fold over at the edges, enclosing a space that will become the inside of the gut.

1. The outside layer of cells, which covers the surface of the embryo, will form the outside layer of the body – the **skin,** the **hair** and **nails** (also the **brain** and **nerves,** see page 28).

2. The inside layer of cells will develop into the lining of the **digestive system,** including the **gut** and digestive organs such as the **liver** and the **pancreas.** It will also form the lining of the **lungs** and the **trachea** (the windpipe).

3. Sandwiched between the other two layers, the middle cell layer develops into all the other parts of the body – the **bones, muscles, heart, blood vessels** and **blood,** and the **connective tissue** that joins all these parts together.

1

2

3

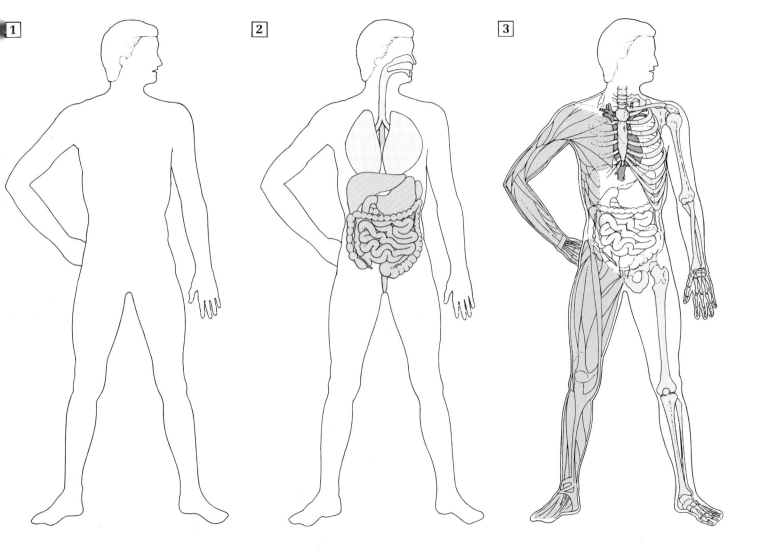

The embryo floats in a pool of liquid within the lining of the mother's uterus. It is nearly three weeks old, but still only 2 mm long. This picture shows the three cell layers, and the streak towards the bottom. In fact the embryo has become pear-shaped, with the head end at the top, and the 'tail end' at the bottom.

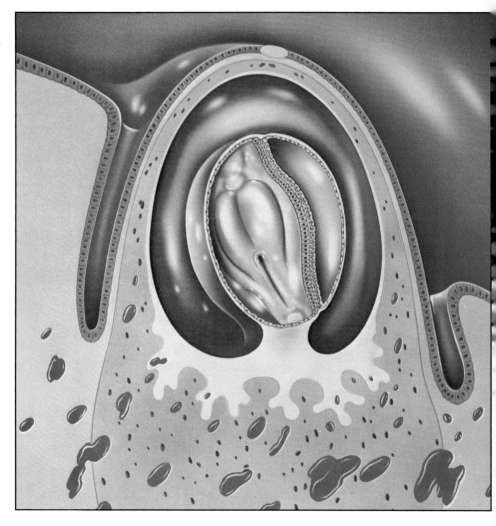

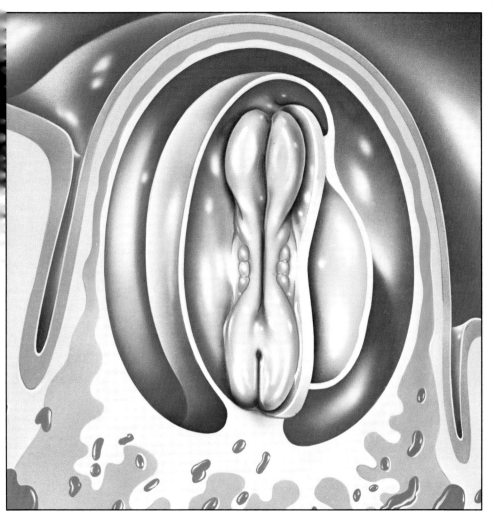

The baby develops 'head first' – that is the head develops first, followed by the body, then the arms and legs. The first part to form is the **brain,** which starts off as two bulges at the head end of the embryo.

The streak has almost disappeared; it can just be seen at the bottom (tail) end. The new furrow which runs the length of the embryo is the beginning of the **spinal cord.**

Two days later, the brain bulges are much larger. The top edges of the furrow join together, forming a tube that will become the centre of the spinal cord. The cells that form the **brain,** the **spinal cord** and the **nerves** are now down inside the embryo, on the inside of the tube. But they come from the same group of cells that covers the surface of the embryo (see page 24).

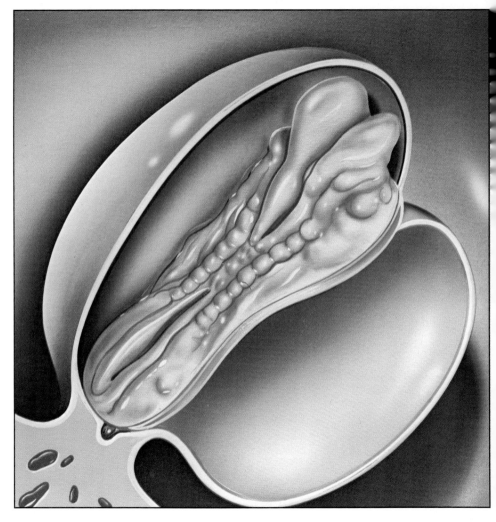

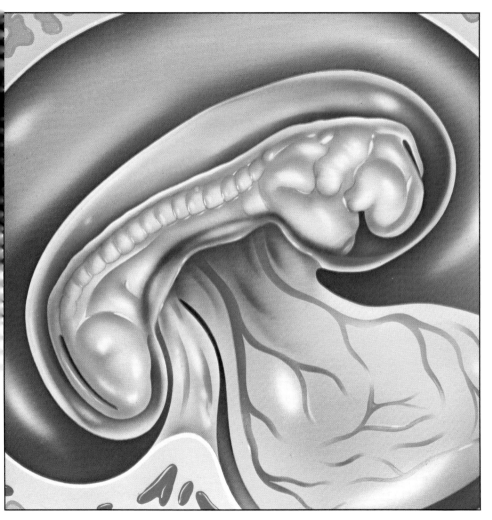

Here we see the embryo from the side, just over three weeks after fertilization. The developing **brain** and **spinal cord** make up most of the embryo at this stage.

Inside the embryo (below), the head and tail ends have folded together, enclosing a space that will become the inside of the **gut** (see page 24). The **heart** has folded into the chest region, and though it is no more than a thickened length of blood vessel, it has already started to beat.

The embryo is still no bigger than a grain of rice. . .

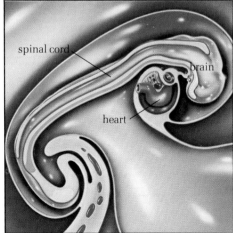

spinal cord

brain

heart

Shaping the parts of the body

The embryo floats in a protective pool of liquid within the wall of the mother's uterus. The yellow balloon-shaped **yolk sac** has begun to make **red blood cells** for the developing blood system.

At this stage, there is little to distinguish a human embryo from the embryo of a monkey, or a rabbit, or any other mammal. There are no arms or legs, and no face or neck. Yet over the next few weeks the embryo will become recognizably human, as cells shape the main parts of the body.

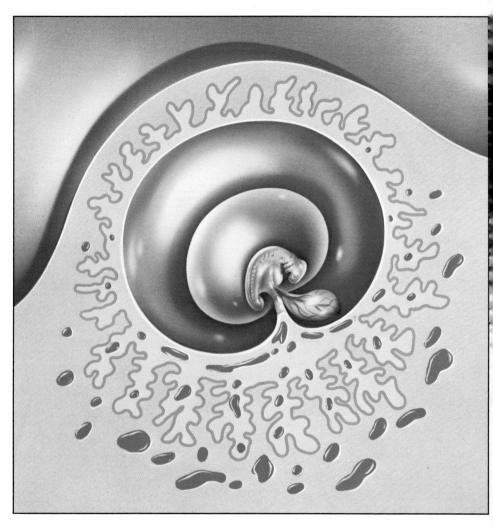

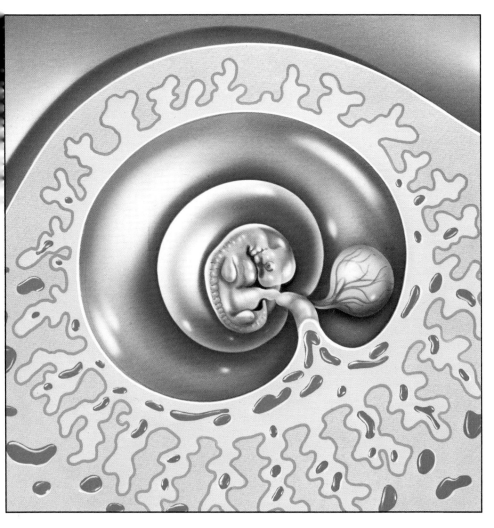

About five weeks after fertilization, the **arms** and **legs** appear as buds growing out of the sides of the body.
The cells in the buds are very active, preparing to develop into the many different kinds of cell that make up an arm or leg – muscle cells, cartilage cells, bone cells, and so on.

One week later, the buds are beginning to look like real arms and legs. Specialized muscle cells develop and group together to form the **muscles** that will soon be able to move the tiny limbs. The **face** has started to form, though the part that looks like the mouth is in fact the developing **ear.** Notice too the bent **neck,** the segmented **back,** and the **tail.**

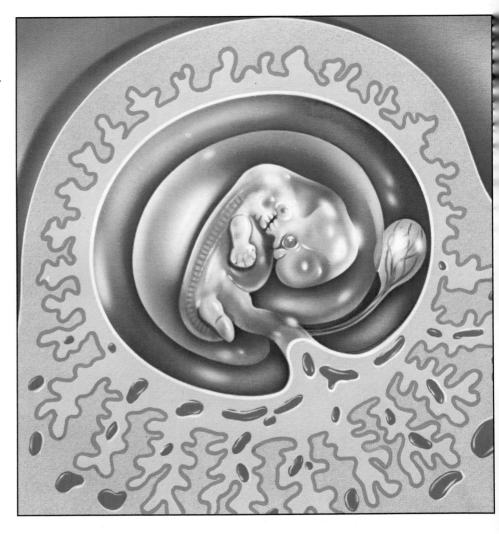

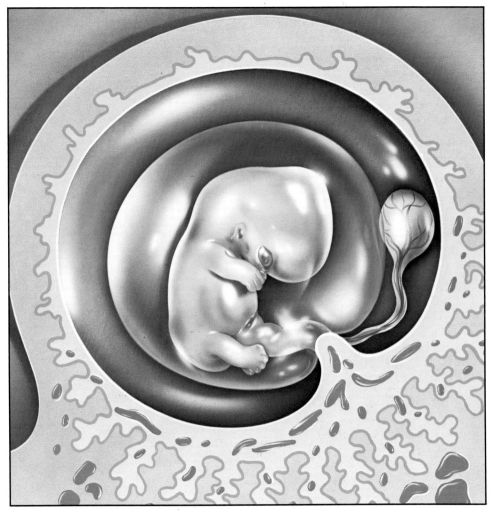

Another week has passed. The back no longer looks segmented, but the divisions are still there underneath the skin – they will develop into the bones of the **spine.** The **eyes** and **ears** have formed, and the **fingers** and **toes** have almost become separated.

Two months after fertilization, the baby is recognizably human. All the main parts of the body have formed, including the **bones,** though they are not yet fully developed. The baby is no longer called an embryo, but is called a **foetus.**
It has taken two months to reach this advanced stage, yet the foetus is only 25 mm long. It will be another seven months before the baby is ready to be born.

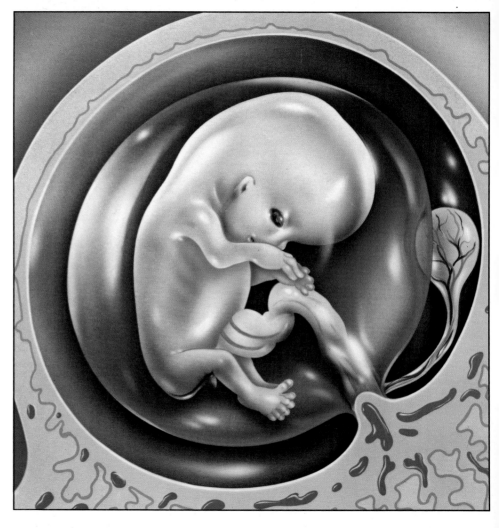

Part three

in which the foetus grows into a baby,
ready to be born

The foetus floats in a pool of liquid, cushioned from sudden movements, bright lights and noise. The cells in its body are still very active, growing and dividing and becoming specialized. Gradually they form the finishing touches such as the **eyelids,** and the **fingernails** and **toenails.**

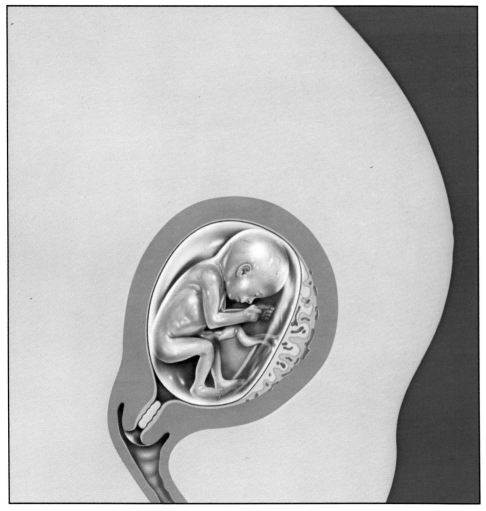

Four months have passed, but there are still five more to go until birth. The baby is now growing very rapidly, about 50 mm each month. The uterus gradually stretches but as the baby grows larger there is less and less room. It is at this stage that the mother's abdomen begins to bulge, and she can feel the baby moving about.

Two or three months before birth, the baby tends to rest head downwards. This is probably the position in which it will be born. The **eyelids,** fused together since the third month, are now open again.

The baby still appears somewhat out of proportion, with a large head and a small body. Over the next two months the body will catch up as the baby grows and puts on fat under the skin.

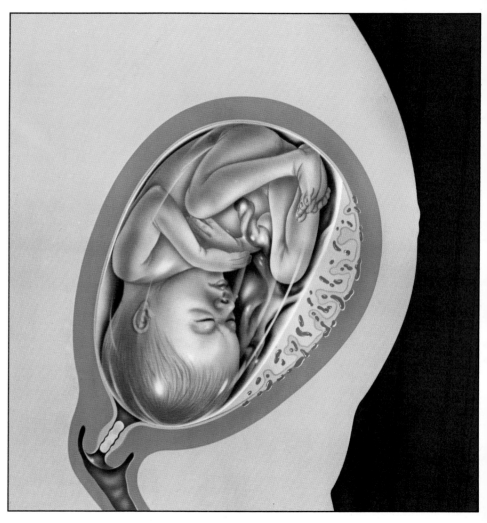

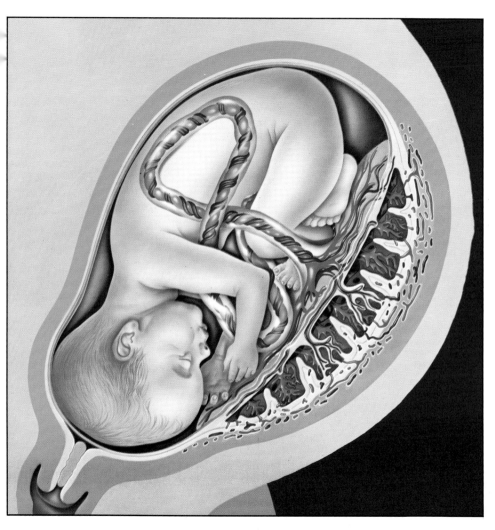

The placenta
– the baby's life-support system.

The placenta is formed partly from cells in the lining of the mother's uterus, and partly from the cells that surround the embryo in the very early stages (see page 16). It is fully developed about three months after fertilization.

How does the placenta work?

The baby's heart pumps blood through the umbilical cord to the placenta. In the placenta, the baby's blood is separated from the mother's blood by a very thin membrane. **Nutrients** and **oxygen** pass through the membrane from the mother's blood to the baby's blood, while **waste products** and **carbon dioxide** pass in the opposite direction and are removed in the mother's blood. The baby's blood then flows back along the umbilical cord, carrying the nutrients and oxygen essential for life.

Nine months have passed, and the baby is at last ready to be born. In the beginning it was a single cell, smaller than a pinhead. Now it is a fully formed baby, made of millions and millions of cells of many different kinds.

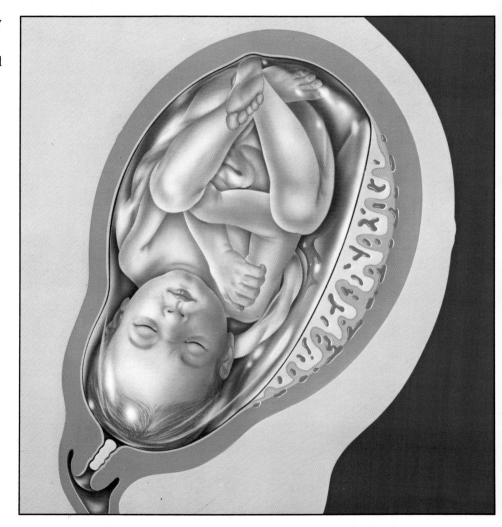

Part four

in which the baby leaves the protection of the uterus, and enters the outside world

Birth

Birth is the first main event in everyone's life. It takes about twelve hours on average, though sometimes it can take much longer, up to thirty hours.

Birth is a very tiring process for both the mother and the baby. It can be divided into three stages – **labour, delivery,** and **afterbirth.**

Labour

This is the longest stage of birth. It starts when the mother feels contractions of the muscles in the uterus wall. The contractions gradually get stronger and more frequent, pushing the baby out of the uterus and into the vagina.

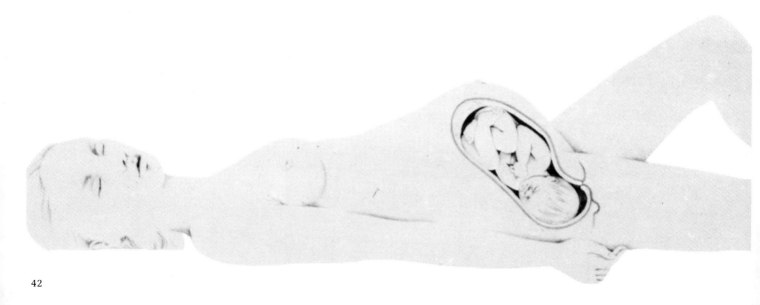

Delivery

The powerful contractions continue, pushing the baby further out of the uterus, until at last the baby's head emerges into the outside world. This is the most difficult and tiring part of birth, but after only a few more contractions the baby is born.

Afterbirth

A few minutes after birth, further contractions of the uterus expel the **placenta.** This is why the placenta is sometimes called the **afterbirth.** After the baby has been born, the placenta is no longer needed, and is removed by cutting through the umbilical cord.

Before the baby is born, it receives nutrients and oxygen from its mother via the placenta (see page 39). The main blood flow is to the placenta and to the baby's body. Very little blood flows to the lungs and digestive system.

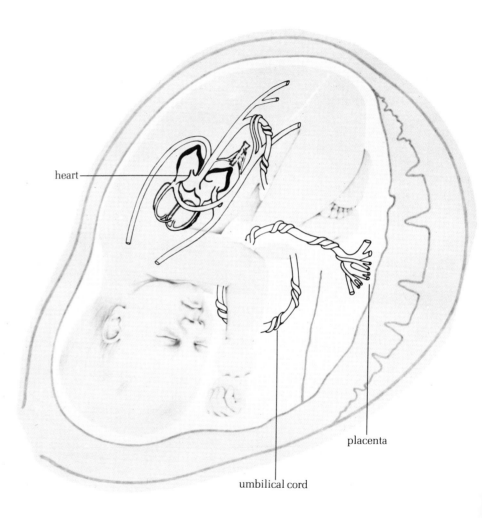

heart

placenta

umbilical cord

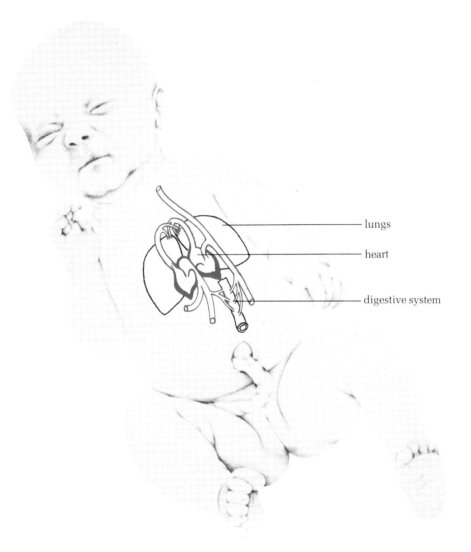

After the baby is born, it breathes in oxygen and starts to eat and digest its own food. The blood circulation changes so that more blood flows to the lungs and digestive system. A knot is tied in the umbilical cord to prevent bleeding. This leaves a scar – the navel ('tummy button').

lungs

heart

digestive system

This has been the story of the first nine
months of life. For this baby, birth day is
the first day of the rest of his life.

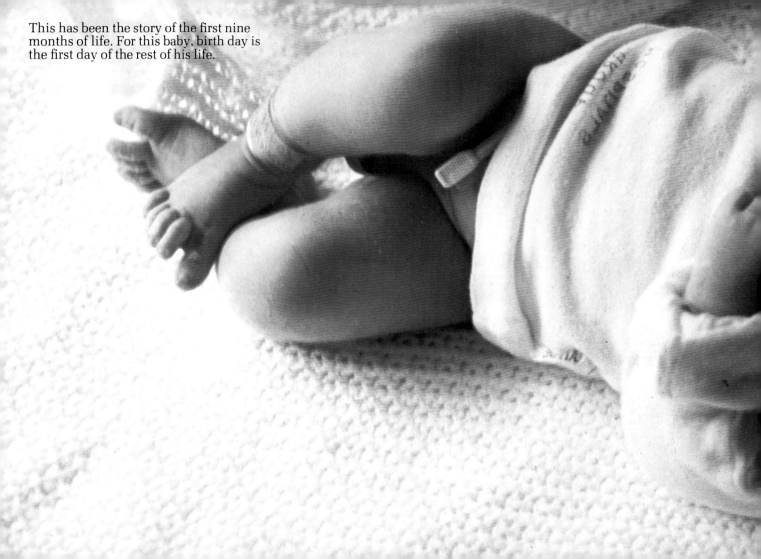

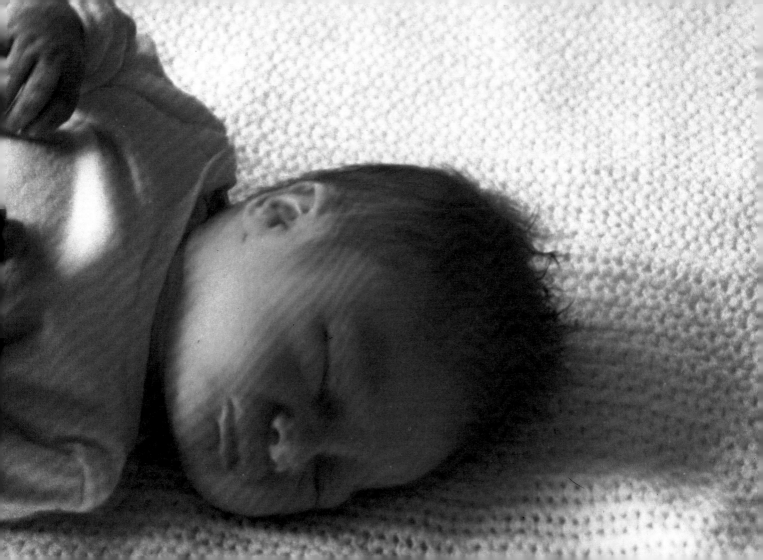

Acknowledgements

Geoff Woods, conception and preliminary illustrations
John Bavosi, colour illustrations pages 10 to 23, 26 to 40
David McGrail, design
Robert Harding Associates, photograph pages 46, 47